A Facilitator's Guide

By Rich Cleveland

Practical training for leading lively and informative small-group discussions

Emmaus Journey
Director: Rich Cleveland
PO Box 63587
Colorado Springs, CO 80962-3587
Telephone: 719-599-0448
Email: info@emmausjourney.org
Web Page: www.emmausjourney.org

ISBN number: 978-0-9785242-3-4

Printed in the United States of America

Copyright 2007 Emmaus Journey

All Rights Reserved

Table of Contents

An Introduction	5
The Importance of Small-Groups	7
The Nature of Small-Groups	14
Choosing the Right Small-Group Track (Focus)	17
Elements of a Successful Small-Group Ministry	22
Developing a Covenantal Relationship	25
Questions, the Key to Generating Discussion	28
Understanding Various Types of Questions	30
Practical Considerations	41
Handling Discussion Group Obstacles	52
A Recap	65

Introduction

A *Facilitator's Guide* is a helpful tool provided by Emmaus Journey to enable small-group facilitators to effectively lead Catholic small-groups. Life is tough, but leading a small-group doesn't have to be. Consequently this particular material is designed to make leading small-groups more enjoyable by providing practical ideas and tips for facilitators that will enhance their ability to lead small-group discussions and make both leading and participating a positive experience.

Rich Cleveland, the founder and director of Emmaus Journey, has trained discussion-group leaders since 1979. From his years of experience, he has selected several key ideas about leading small-group discussions, which he believes are especially beneficial in making facilitation of small-groups more simple and enjoyable.

Does a a small-group need a facilitator?

Perhaps you have observed that many Catholic small-groups elect to share the facilitating responsibilities. You probably have also observed that quite often when a group is led by an untrained facilitator it is a less than enjoyable and productive experience.

We cannot imagine giving our retirement money to an untrained investment broker, or using a doctor who only desires to practice medicine but who has never received any hands on practical training. Why then should we be willing to entrust the spiritual enthusiasm and formation of those who chose to participate in small-groups to the leadership of someone who does not know what they are doing when it comes to facilitating a small-group. Invariably when we use an untrained leader we are setting up the leader and the small-group for a disappointing and perhaps even harmful experience.

A well trained facilitator is of great value in leading a small-group. A person need not be an expert in Scripture or Church doctrine, although some knowledge of both will be helpful. The reason for this is that the facilitator does not function as a teacher. The facilitator's primary responsibilities are to keep the group focused on the particular topic, to see that each person in the group has an opportunity to participate, and to keep the group discussions moving forward. For this reason we recommend that every small-group should be led by a trained facilitator. If a group insists on sharing the facilitating duties, then simply insure that prior to starting the small-group each person participates in adequate training. At the very least each person should have an opportunity to discuss and digest with others the content of this booklet.

With the need for practical training in mind and a desire that small-groups and their facilitators have a enjoyable and successful experience we offer the following proven principles and techniques.

The Importance of Small-Groups

During the last several decades the Catholic Church has observed a perplexing problem. Thousands and thousands of our young people and young adults have left the Catholic Church primarily in search of the Bible. Frequently, the primary lure is an invitation to participate in an effective and informative small-group bible study. Then falling afresh in love with God's Scripture and the people who make studying it available to them they unconsciously drift from the Church into Protestantism. This should not be so. Why should members of the Roman Catholic Church, who have throughout history been the preservers of Holy Scripture, determiners of the Canon of Scripture, and interpreters of orthodox truth, have to leave the Church to find an environment where they can study and discuss sacred Scripture?

Some have expressed to me a fear that if people engage in small-group bible study without a priest present they will slip into heresy. In over forty years of experience leading small-groups and working with people who lead small-groups I have not seen that happen. On the contrary, invariably the people who slip into heresy usually have preceded their slide by withdrawing from fellow Christians who can help balance out their misconceptions. The Holy Spirit is not dead. He is alive and active doing very well those tasks for which he was sent to us, one of which is very pertinent to this point, namely, to guide us into truth:

> "But the Counselor, the Holy Spirit, whom the Father will send in my name, he will teach you all things, and bring to your remembrance all that I have said to you." John 14:26

> "When the Spirit of truth comes, he will guide you into all the truth, for he will not speak on his own authority, but whatever he hears he will speak, and he will declare to you the things that are to come." John 16:13

The Holy Spirit is faithful to lead his holy people into understanding, understanding that is consistent with

Church teachings, when they come together to study and discuss Holy Scripture.

Encouragingly, throughout the Church there is a new awareness of the need to respond to these desires and to provide effective and informative small-group bible studies from within Catholic parishes. Increasingly Catholic leaders are encouraging people to participate in bible study small-groups, and increasingly providing excellent and stimulating small-group bible study materials. For instance as early as 1992 the National Conference of Catholic Bishops was suggesting evangelization goals which included:

> "To foster an appreciation of God's word in the lives of all Catholics
>
> Possible strategies:
>
> - more frequent individual reading of the Bible among Catholics;
> - the further development of scriptural-study and scriptural-sharing programs; and
> - opportunities for more thorough scriptural studies on the part of all Catholics. ..."
>
> And, "To foster active and personal religious experience through participation in small-group and other communal experiences in which the Good News is shared, experienced, and applied to daily life."[1]

In addition Pope John Paul II speaking of small-groups said, "These communities are a sign of vitality within the Church, an instrument of formation and evangelization, and a solid starting point for a new society based on a 'civilization of love.'"[2]

If further evidence of the value of small-groups is desired, we need only look to the life and methodology of our Lord Jesus. As you will recall, though he spoke to large crowds, the crux of his ministry involved inviting a small group of twelve men to accompany him. "... Jesus showed us that a

---

[1] *Go and Make Disciples: A National Plan and Strategy for Catholic Evangelization in the United States*

[2] *Mission of the Redeemer*

radically new relationship is possible between God and humans and among human beings. It is a relationship of integrity, wholeness, and freedom from fear and anxiety. It is a relationship of justice and peace. It is the coming of the reign of God.

"Following Jesus in the power of the Spirit requires a conversion according to the scriptural word. Our attitudes, our values, our commitments need to be in accord with the call and teaching of Jesus Christ. Strength is provided us through prayer, the sacramental life, and our commitment to community life."[3]

This a good description of what small-groups are all about; "conversion according to the scriptural word." These words from *Small Christian Communities: A Vision of Hope* speak of the possibility of transformation that is available to people through small-groups of believers united to study and apply sacred Scripture and becoming formed into a faith community.

Someone has said that the distance between a sterile, ineffectual knowledge of faith and a vital, life-changing faith is about 17 inches—that's the distance between our head and our heart. A well-facilitated small-group discussion will enable an individual to turn off his "ahuh" and begin to really consider the claims of Christ on his/her life. Well-directed questions and lively discussion causes a person to *think*, many for the first time, of what it means to be a Catholic Christian in the world today. Once the Holy Spirit has a person's attention, he is able to bring about transformation from the inside out.

Our Lord's ministry is an ideal illustration of the value of small-group discussion. He gathered around him 12 men and engaged them in dialog about what it meant to be a participant in the Kingdom of God. Jesus formed his disciples by asking questions that caused them to reevaluate who he was and what they were called to be. (See Matthew 16:13–20, or John 6:60–62, 67–69.)

Well-facilitated small-group discussions can:

- Provide an incentive and motivation for people to

---

3 *Small Christian Communities: A Vision of Hope,* (Paulist Press) page 39

reflect more deeply on their relationship with Jesus Christ, his call on their lives, and how they are to live out this call.

- Encourage people to prepare and study together topics of importance to their faith, a study that is probably more thorough than they would do on their own.

- Help people to form and/or strengthen convictions more rapidly as they discuss and learn together and support one another in living out these convictions.

- Plumb the depths of the practical implications of scriptural truths and Church teachings for Catholics, and enable people to develop and live a fuller expression of their faith in the context of other like-minded individuals.

- Provide a pleasant and constructive environment that encourages people to learn from one another and press forward in their quest for spiritual maturity.

- Create a check and balance against aberrant and harmful private interpretation that could lead them and others away from Christ and his Church.

One Place Where It Happened

Our Lady, Queen of Martyrs Parish in Woonsocket, Rhode Island—Developing a Creative Solution

Fr. Maurice Brindamour and Ghislaine Parenteau came up with a unique solution for meeting parishoners' needs. After a memorable year long 50th Jubilee of Our Lady, Queen of Martyrs Parish, Ghislaine, a few months short of her eightieth birthday, felt a need for "revitalization" and she suspected that she was not alone with these feelings. Consequently, she talked with Father "Moe" (Fr. Maurice Brindamour) and suggested starting a bible study as a solution.

Fr. Brindamour recognized that adult education and formation had been neglected in the past but because he was only months into this new parish assignment only promised, "I'll think about it." He was aware that the parishioners needed and wanted the facilitator/instructor to be someone who had studied the Scriptures, and he wasn't sure he would have the time to do it. In addition he "wasn't interested in just an 'academic' approach to the subject of God's Word.

Fr. Maurice Brindamour and Ghislaine Parenteau

I wanted a pastoral, spiritual approach that would invite people to apply the Holy Scriptures … What is God saying to us and to me? How has the word been preached to people in the past and is the message relevant to me/us today? Can a Catholic read the Bible with confidence and understand it and apply it without misinterpreting its meaning? …I was convinced that a small group sharing type setting was the best way for adults to form their own opinions about how God is speaking to them"

Through The Word Among Us' monthly devotional magazine, Ghislaine had done her homework and found the Emmaus Journey bible study and facilitator's guide for *Serving the Master.* In addition she already had found ten parishioners who were eager to participate. With Father's "Yes," they were off and running with a core group of over twenty people. Speaking of *Serving the Master,* Fr. Brindamour says, "I was attracted to this study since it was topical (keeping one theme), spiritually challenging, and deeply scripturally based. It is a topic that every pastor is interested in fostering in parishioners. ... But most of all it was very dynamic in that it called everyone to participate and share their opinions."

After a successful study with 20–40 people participating, Ghislaine suggested that they study *Living in the Power of the Holy Spirit,* also an Emmaus Journey study published by The Word Among Us. This study also received another overwhelmingly enthusiastic response from approximately forty people. She explains, "This study has been an awakening for all of us. We came to realize that when the Spirit moves, we better be ready to act! The Holy Spirit inspires us to be bold as the first disciples were. ... This particular Bible study brought us together as brothers and sisters, made us more conscious of the gifts of the Holy Spirit, helped us to develop them, to welcome them, and to use them for the good of ourselves and the Church, and for the good of the world. Many of us found ourselves awaiting the Pentecost in a way never before experienced."

An additional result, according to Fr. Brindamour, is that "people began talking to other friends, neighbors and relatives about their study." Another local pastor "hearing about our success, has asked to include his parishioners in the program. And so we'll be trying to expand this opportunity to his people. If we get a response, Fr. Gerry Finnegan, pastor of St. Charles parish, will be the co-facilitator with me in the third series."

This story of small-group bible study at Our Lady, Queen of Martyrs Parish is a story of one person, who had never attended a bible study and her desire to experience Christ more fully. And also of a pastor's desire to respond to that need by making sacred Scripture relevant and available to his parishioners, in spite of a very busy schedule. These two desires came together in a most creative way—a monthly study that is enlivening those who participate and stimulating both community and mission.

Our Lady, Queen of Martyrs Parish is seeing results that any parish would love to see, "We have couples with adult children looking for a way to reflect on their vocation as parents and grandparents; a Catholic high school teacher who continues her thirst for knowledge and faith; a young married couple who are searching to make their faith real. And of course we have seniors living on their own who find spiritual stimulation not only from God's Word but also a real sense of belonging to the larger family of God's people gathered around the table of His Word and his sacred food." May God multiply these affects, "a deeper relationship with the Lord and a deeper sense of Christian community," in hundreds of parishes.

The Nature of Small-Groups

Obviously, the kind of small-groups we will be talking about are by nature different than what Jesus did, but nevertheless vitally important. The definition I like best to describe what we are going to be talking about is, "A Christian small group is an intentional face-to-face gathering of three to twelve people on a regular time schedule with a common purpose of discovering and growing in the possibilities of abundant life in Christ."[4] Let's look at each element of this definition.

- **Intentional**—It is important that the participants of the small-group have a healthy understanding of the purpose for which they are meeting. Someone has wisely said that if you aim at nothing you'll hit it every time. This is so true. When there is a confusion of objectives and purposes people will endeavor to take the small-group in different directions, and dissatisfaction and discontent will often set in.

  The small-group should also be intentional by being designed to intentionally develop and form people as Christ's disciples—to help move them from where they are spiritually to where they want and ought to be spiritually. Discipleship does not happen by accident but should involve a well thought out, reproducible plan, that establishes people in their relationship with Christ and his Church and mobilizes them in mission for Christ and his Church. (*A Vision for Ministry: Seeing more clearly the potential and process of forming Catholic disciples*[5] is an excellent resource to share with your leaders to help them understand the intentional, disciple-forming aspects of facilitating a small-group.)

---

4 Attributed to Roberta Hestenes, source unknown.

5 Available from Emmaus Journey

- **Face-to-face**—Small-groups are designed for interpersonal relationships. When facilitated effectively both the interaction within the group and the interaction among participants outside of the group will create a chemistry that will result in deep interpersonal relationships—friendships if you will, that will continue to endure long after the small-group concludes.

- **Three to twelve people**—The size of an effective small-group is determined by the amount of time you have for discussion. Since small-groups are not the place for teaching lectures but for multi-level discussion, if less than three people are involved you simply end up with a person-to-person dialog. If more than twelve people are involved there is not adequate time for everyone to meaningfully participate.

For instance if you have twelve people in a sixty minute discussion each person only has a maximum of four minutes to speak—actually less time than that when you factor in the time necessary to facilitate and to read the bible study questions and Scripture references.

Small-groups are based on successful adult learning characteristics. For instance: Large groups tend to be to impersonal in both their presentation and focus, whereas one-to-one is often too intense for many adults. Small-groups on the other hand provide a high level of interpersonal relationships which contributes to both learning and application of truth. It is a proven fact that adults learn best in community and of the three methods of pedagogy (large groups, small groups, and one-to-one) small-groups provide the best community environment. In addition adults tend to motivate one another.

Adults primarily learn by discovery not by instruction, or telling. Small-groups, with effective materials and facilitation, provide the best environment for discovery. Additionally, the discovery process is amplified as a group of people share and discuss what they have discovered with the rest of the group, thus allowing the discovery process to not only take place in the preparation but also within the discussion.

Of the three methods of pedagogy small-groups best prevent the problem of the privatization of religion. In an environment where your ideas and understanding is shared and discussed with other Catholics, any misunderstanding or incorrect interpretation has a better chance of being rectified and balanced by the input from fellow group members. In both the one speaker monologue and one-on-one dialog, opportunities for doctrinal imbalance are enhanced.

- **Regular time schedule**—Small-groups can meet weekly, biweekly, or monthly, but the effectiveness diminishes in relationship to the gap that exists between meetings. We recommend that small-groups meet weekly for anywhere from eight to twelve weeks, and then take a healthy break before resuming. Biweekly and monthly meeting schedules make it more difficult to maintain continuity with the material and build relationship with the other participants.

- **Common purpose of discovering and growing**—This element introduces the primary way adults learn, through the discovery of truth. Later we will give some helpful information on how to create this atmosphere of discovery, but for now it is simply important to reiterate that the group must have this as their agreed upon purpose.

- **Direct investigation of Scripture**—This is an element I would add to the above definition and will be the context in which we will explain these small-group facilitating principles and techniques. This takes us back to our starting place on the importance of small-groups. Catholics need, and desire to know and be able to explain their faith in the context of sacred Scripture. Effective small-group bible studies, and effective small-group bible study materials are ones which enable Catholics to open their Bibles and directly investigate—read and think about—sacred Scripture.

Choosing the Right Small-Group Track (Focus)

There are various kinds of small-group bible studies. Most parishes have organized their small-groups around a main track on which their ministry runs or revolves. Usually this main track becomes the backbone of your small-group ministry and shapes both the direction of the small-groups and the participants you attract.

Usually a parish's main track will fit in one of the following categories:

- **Purpose Driven Small-groups**—These are small-groups usually designed to answer the question, "What do you want the bible study to accomplish?" Frequently this purpose is decided by the parish leadership and fits within the context of the larger mission and goals of the parish.

    Perhaps some examples of *purpose driven* small-groups would be those that are designed:

    - to provide a shepherding or care component,
    - to prevent attrition and provide for the assimilation of new people,
    - to form people in the fundamentals of their faith, or
    - to provide focused information, such as natural family planning.

- **Need or Interest Driven Small-groups**—These small-groups usually answer the question, "What kind of small-groups do people feel they need and are asking to have?" These kinds of small-groups usually are preceded by the statement, "We need _____ to help solve the problem of _____." They are focused on meeting felt needs of the individuals who are asking for them. Their point of origination is usually from within the potential participants, rather than from leadership. They are designed to meet felt needs rather than being mission based.

Some examples of *interest or need driven* small-groups are groups that will help us:

- experience community,
- learn the Bible,
- understand concepts like Christian marriage, or
- deal with issues like social justice

- **Program Driven Small-groups**—Are those that answer the question, "What proven small-group program will we use." They can be originated either by leadership, by participants, or by the program's promoters. They may or may not be consistent with the parish's mission or specifically designed to meet participants' felt needs. Usually they are a successful or popular form/format that others are using which we hope will give us similar results.

Some examples of these are:

- Renew 2000
- Disciples in Mission
- Emmaus Journey Series
- Little Rock Series

All of these and other programs are excellent materials, but if the program is not selected in light of the parishes *purposes* or in light of meeting people's *felt needs* they may or may not be successful. Ideally, which ever track your small-group ministry runs on, the leadership should go out of their way to guarantee success. Once a small-group track is successfully established then a parish can branch out to develop other types of small-groups.

One Place Where It Happened

Abe and Liz Chavez along with a team of several couples have helped conduct and manage Marriage Enrichment Retreats at Holy Rosary Parish. A couple interesting aspects of Marriage Enrichment is that it is primarily run by a team of lay people, and the participants process the information they are learning in small discussion groups. By the end of the retreat people have become comfortable with the small-group format and usually find that they really enjoy the sharing environment. Because the team desires to provide ongoing formation for those who attend they frequently end the retreat with the statement, "If you have enjoyed the discussion group format you have experienced here this weekend we invite you to become part of one of the small-groups that meets on a regular basis."

Holy Rosary Parish in Albuquerque, NM— Retreats Provide a Springboard to Small-Groups

Abe and Liz Chavez

Why the focus on small-groups? In the words of Abe and Liz, "We have found them invaluable for staying sharp and staying focused on one's journey with God. We have seen the value of sharing and growing alongside of others who also desire to become more intimate in their relationship with God. Also in this environment we are able to care for and encourage one another to grow the Kingdom of God in our souls."

In addition the community aspect of small-groups is very important, "One of the values of the Kingdom of God is becoming family. A small-group provides an excellent environment where individuals experience 'family' as we share our joys, sorrows, and challenges along with a commitment to love and support one another." Whether people in the small-group community at Holy Rosary are celebrating a wedding, graduation, or other event, or simply trying to weather difficult crises like a death, severe illness, or unexpected job loss, the love and support of the community is there for them actively involved praying, helping, being with them in the midst of either the joy or sorrow.

In recent years, the ACTS Ministry has been introduced to Holy Rosary. At these retreats the men and women involved go to separate retreats where they are called to Christ and encouraged through Adoration, Community, Theology and Service to re-embrace their baptismal vows. But we all know how easy it is to make commitments in the holy environment of a spiritual retreat. The difficulty is how to help people live out their commitments after the retreat. It is through small-groups that the spiritual momentum of the retreat is maintained. This is where real growth happens and where love and caring touch daily life. Consequently, out of every ACTS Retreat the goal is to start one or more new small-groups.

Typical is one woman's story. She was a cradle Catholic who never really understood her faith or knew why she believed what she believed. The retreat was meaningful for her so she joined the small-group where various important topics were covered and where sacred Scripture broadened her vision and helped her understand what being a Catholic means. In the last two years she has grown so much that even the discussion of more complex issues leaves her excited about her faith and willing to share it with others. The growth experienced through the small-group has caused her to serve in other ways in the parish, including serving as a team member for the next ACTS Women's Retreat.

The Chavez' rely on effective small-group materials many of which come from Emmaus Journey. For instance for some time they relied on *Reflecting On Sunday's Readings,* which is a free small-group bible study tied to the Mass readings and available from Emmaus Journey. In addition they have successfully used other Emmaus Journey studies like *The Seven Last Words of Christ.* They explain, "It is very helpful when you have good, written resources to facilitate the process. The materials from Emmaus Journey are excellent and foster good thought, discussion, and application of what we are learning."

At Holy Rosary through small-groups and person-to-person ministry people are being encouraged and challenged to embrace Christ more deeply. In the midst of their small-group community there are many who are able to model their faith as an example for others, while serving one another in love.

Elements of a successful small-group ministry

When analyzing parishes that have developed successful small-group ministries, several elements consistently emerge that are present in most of them. Parishes and small-group coordinators should give special attention to insure that the following elements are present.

1. **Clear Vision or Purpose**

    In light of the above information it is essential that the leadership of the parish and those interested in facilitating small-groups be on the same page in their thinking about what they are trying to accomplish, and why. Annually, there should be a time for assessing the results of your small-group ministry efforts to see if they are accomplishing your purpose and meeting needs. This annual assessment will enable you to make adjustments to both your vision and your activities.

2. **Pastoral Support**

    People tend to rise to the expectations that are placed upon them. If participation in the small-groups of the parish is presented as just one of many things people in the parish can do then small-groups will be relegated to a less important place in people's minds and priorities. The pastoral staff's public support is crucial to the success of the parish's small-group ministry. People need to hear, again and again, the leader of the parish emphasizing that participating in small-groups is a good and important thing for them to do.

    People should hear the pastoral staff commend those who are facilitating and those who are participating in small-groups and in a public way allude to the value small-groups are having in people's lives. Pastors should verbally help with the recruiting by recommending and encouraging participation in small-groups both from the pulpit, or in personal counseling. Pastoral staff should insure that the parish budget includes money for training and materials, and that a small-group coordinator is appointed to be a part of the parish leadership team. When these kinds of steps are taken by the pastoral staff they will help insure that the small-group ministry thrives.

3. **Viewed as a Means Not an End**

   Small-groups are a method of teaching, a means to accomplish specific purposes or meet specific needs such as leading people to conversion, forming them as disciples, equipping them with needed information or skills. We shouldn't do small-groups just to be doing small-groups or to simply follow the example of some other church. For small-groups to receive the attention they need to be effective they cannot be just another add-on activity. They should be a tool we selectively utilize to accomplish a specific *purpose,* or to meet a specific *need* or *interest.*

4. **Trained Leadership**

   We have already spoken briefly about the need to adequately train everyone who will be facilitating a small-group. Allowing small-groups to be led by untrained facilitators will inevitably lead to the demise of the small-group, or in the co-opting of the small-group's agenda. In addition to the initial facilitators training, the small-group coordinator for the parish should schedule annual refresher evenings where facilitators are reminded of important principles and/or provided with additional insights on how to lead the material you are using. Though a trained facilitator might not need to participate in a facilitators' meeting monthly, at least once or twice a year it is helpful to bring the facilitators together to discuss ideas, resolve problems, introduce new material, answer questions, etc.

5. **Participants' Commitment**

   If the parish, the pastor, and the facilitators are all committed to working diligently and with excellence to do their part to make small-groups effective, yet the participants have not been called to a similarly high standard, long-range success will be jeopardized.

One of my favorite thought provoking sayings is, "Though you're only young once, you can remain immature indefinitely." Somehow we allow the concept to exist that spiritual immaturity and immature behavior is acceptable in the Church, when it would not be accepted or tolerated anywhere else. In a gracious loving way we need to help participants understand that we expect them to attend unless there is an emergency and to thoroughly complete their assignments, and with a positive attitude. Most employers, and membership based groups would expect and accept nothing less. Being a member of Christ's Church, a member of a Catholic parish, and a member of a small-group is a privilege which demands as high or higher commitment. When it is there, the benefits and effectiveness of a small-group are off the chart.

6. **Effective Spiritual Resources**

    A really good facilitator can make even inadequate materials succeed, but new and developing facilitators can often be undermined by having inadequate materials. Effective small-group bible study materials should contain an element of discovery, not indoctrination. As we have pointed out this is the way most adults learn, by discovery.

Effective small-group bible study materials should contain well thought-out questions that lead to understanding rather than simply provide instruction and information. The reason it is a bible *study* is that it should require effort to research, think about, and arrive at your own conclusions and application—which when done in a parish small-group environment will be consistent with the Church's teachings. The difference is that instead of the information simply going from someone else's head to your notebook page, bible *study* requires it to pass through the reasoning process of your mind, being better understood and more effectively retained. So take the necessary effort to find Catholic materials that work.

Developing a Covenantal Relationship

Earlier we talked about the importance of securing a high level commitment from the small-group participants. We want to be able to do this in parish environments where high level commitment may not be normative, and do it in a positive and effective way.

Some small-group training resources speak of developing a small-group "covenant" that asks participants to commit to a set of agreed upon parameters. The value of having a covenantal relationship is that it enables participants to avoid many misunderstandings and assumptions. The covenantal agreement clearly states how the group will function and what is expected of a participant. Unfortunately, this normally involves a rather laborious process that consist of:

- **Identifying issues which need to be resolved;**
  - Purpose of the group,
  - How the group will be organized,
  - The nature and culture of the group,
  - Commitment expectations and responsibilities.
- **Clearly stating any non-negotiables.**
- **Discussing and agreeing on each point.**
- **Word-smithing the covenant.**
- **Producing and distributing a final agreement.**

At best it would take one complete session to adequately start from scratch and develop this kind of an agreement. More often it will take more time than that. Most people when they sign up for a small-group are not interested in going through such a laborious process, consequently we recommend simply using a commitment card.

Here is how it works. In advance of the orientation meeting the facilitator, or perhaps the parish facilitator team, prepares a "Small-Group Covenant" card similar to the one on the next page.

During your first evening together the facilitator should say something like, "Let's take a few minutes and talk about our commitments to one another. I have taken some time to prepare a card that explains what I feel my minimum commitments should be to each of you individually and as a group." Then give one of these cards to each individual so they can follow along as you explain and perhaps amplify on each point. For instance on the first point, "To be present weekly except in case of emergency," you could say something like, "We all have times when we have a bad week, when we might be out of sorts, or tired, or unprepared, or having company. But I do not have the right, and should not take the liberty at the last minute, to cancel the bible study because I am feeling less than 100%. If I'm really sick or contagious that is one thing, but a slight headache or feeling in a bad mood isn't a legitimate reason to not show up. So I'm committed to being here each week."

> **St. Mary's Parish**
> **Small-Group Facilitator Covenant**
>
> **Your Facilitator's Commitment to you:**
> To be present weekly except incase of an emergency
> To communicate any changes promptly
> To attend with each lesson thoroughly prepared
> To prepare in advance to lead effectively and graciously
> To start and end the meetings on time
> To participate with openness and to be teachable
> To pray for you and for the group's success
> To hold what is said here in confidence

As you amplify on these points, explaining what you will and won't do as their facilitator you are also illustrating by example how they should think about their commitments as well. So quickly work your way through your list of commitments to them. When you are finished, ask, "Are there any other things I should consider?" and then listen to their feedback.

Once you have finished discussing your commitments say something like, "Let's take just a few minutes to discuss what commitments you think we should make to one another. Please turn the card over, break into groups of three and quickly list what you believe are valid considerations. Here are some areas you can consider: Commitments regarding attendance, interpersonal communication, preparation, participation, and anything else you think is important." Then give them 5–6 minutes to develop their list.

After they are finished take a large pad or sheet of paper and develop a composite list that people can agree upon. Don't waste a lot of time getting the wording perfect, but simply capture the idea. Once you have a general consensus of the group's thinking, reiterate the points they listed. If you feel that they overlooked some important point you can suggest it to them. Then with good eye contact with the group participants ask, "Is this a list of commitments that you feel you can all agree upon?" If you have agreement, ask your assistant to come back next week with a clear articulation of what they have agreed upon.

Return to the second session with a well designed commitment card which you should give to each person. As you distribute the cards simply ask, "Have we captured the intentions you talked about last week? Are we comfortable with this and in agreement?" If so, then thank them and express the thought that if we maintain and fulfill these commitments we can be assured that God will do significant things in our lives during this small-group study. The following is an example of a finished group covenant.

St. Mary's Parish Small-Group Participant's Covenant

We agree to:
Make weekly participation a priority in our lives
Endeavor to attend with the lessons well prepared
Commit to learn in a spirit of openness and humility
Listen and share responsibly
Seek the Holy Spirit's guidance
Arrive on time
Share in the hospitality responsibilities
Maintain confidentiality with one another

Questions, the Key to Generating Discussion

One of the keys to having a lively and stimulating discussion in a Catholic small-group is asking good questions. This is especially important for you as facilitator, but all members of a small-group bear some responsibility for asking good questions of one another.

Your first objective as facilitator is to get people thinking. Only then does the second objective of communicating life-changing truth come into play. The most well developed presentation becomes ineffectual if the listener has turned on their "ahuh," and is not listening, or if they are so busy taking notes that they cannot think and digest what is being said. If you turn these objectives around, you will find yourself *instructing* people rather than devising ways to help them *discover* truth. "A living faith is a searching faith—it *'seeks understanding.'* Adults need to question, probe, and critically reflect on the meaning of God's revelation in their unique lives in order to grow closer to God."[6]

Telling is not teaching, as any parent will affirm. Telling tends to cut the learning process short whereas well-developed questions seem to enhance the learning process and stimulate people's desire to know. If you raise a timely, well-thought-out question and allow people to wrestle with the answer, the truth will become part of their understanding.

There are many question formats you can use. But before we explain some of these formats it helps to understand the process of preparing and using questions. Here is the sequence I recommend.

1. Prepare the bible study lesson for your own enlightenment as a fellow participant.

2. Review the material for words, concepts, and implications that would be helpful to have expanded and clarified.

3. Decide which type of question format would best

---

6 *Our Hearts Were Burning Within Us*, paragraph 52

enable others to think through on the word, concept, or implication. It is always more interesting if you use a variety of question formats.

4. Compose the question and write it in the margin of the bible study or resource material you are studying so that during the discussion it will be readily available if needed. Always compose many more questions than you anticipate using.

5. During the discussion, based on the group's interest and understanding of the material (and when needed), selectively use those questions that will stimulate discussion.

Learning to ask effective questions is the key to getting participants involved discussing their understanding of the material you are studying. Questions are often the key to unlocking understanding in the minds of those in a small-group. By asking effective questions it forces the answerer to process the information and arrive at the understanding in their own mind. If you use this sequence when preparing to facilitate a small-group session you will find yourself relaxed and having adequate questions to explore the material and keep the group involved.

Jesus' Use of Questions

We see the value of questions in the life and ministry of Jesus. He had for sometime explained and demonstrated that he had come from the Father and was the only way to the Father. The disciples and those who listened to and observed him were growing in their information about him, but Jesus used a series of questions, as we can see in the following passage, to enable Peter and the other disciples to process the information they had been gathering and come to a meaningful conclusion.

> **Luke 16:13-17**
>
> [13]Now when Jesus came into the district of Caesare'a Philip'pi, he asked his disciples, **"Who do men say that the Son of man is?"**
>
> [14]And they said, "Some say John the Baptist, others say Eli'jah, and others Jeremiah or one of the prophets."
>
> [15]He said to them, **"But who do you say that I am?"**
>
> [16]Simon Peter replied, "You are the Christ, the Son of the living God."
>
> [17]And Jesus answered him, "Blessed are you, Simon Bar-Jona! For flesh and blood has not revealed this to you, but my Father who is in heaven. [18]And I tell you, you are Peter, and on this rock I will build my church, and the powers of death shall not prevail against it."

Understanding Various Types of Questions

If you go to a bookstore that sells bible studies and look through the available resource material you will discover that the questions written therein usually fall into one of three categories; questions of observation, questions of understanding, and questions of application or implication.

- **Observation Questions** are usually the predominant type of questions utilized in most books. This type of question primarily asks, "What do you see within the text?" For instance if you were studying the fruit of the Spirit in Galatians 5:22–23 an observation question might be, "What attitudes or behaviors are listed as characteristics of the Holy Spirit?" A person would then simply read this passage and record from their Bible into their bible study booklet the characteristics listed there. Observation questions provide the basis on which other questions, ones that are designed to enable them to process this information, can be asked.

- **Understanding Questions** ask the question, "What do the things you have observed mean?" A good understanding question enables a person to start examining the ramifications of the discovery they have made from observing the text accurately. In the small-group discussion is where you should spend the majority of your time, helping participants express what they understand from the material they have been studying. Using, for example, the same passage from Galatians 5:22–23, a good understanding questions might be, "Of the nine characteristics mentioned which one do you feel is most important?" or "Why are these things called 'fruit' of the Holy Spirit?"

- **Application or Implication Questions** ask the question, "What do these things mean to me?" or "How should I respond in light of this information?" The Holy Spirit uses some things we study to bring about an immediate application, something that we need to *do* in light of what was studied. For instance realizing in the above passage that self-control should be a characteristic of our life in Christ, and recalling that we recently lost our temper against someone in our family, the Holy Spirit might have us make the application of going to that person and apologize and ask their forgiveness. Other passages may not invoke something that we need to immediately *do* but rather something we need to *keep in mind* or remember in the future. These are implications. For instance if you were studying the same passage above and realize that these characteristics come from the Holy Spirit and not simply from self-effort, you might be reminded to continually ask for the infilling of the Holy Spirit.

Many of these application/implication questions are not included in most of the small-group bible study resources available on the market. Consequently, you may have to write these types of questions yourself. Often the ones that are written are too specific or are pushing toward a very specific kind of application. Remember that sacred Scripture was not written to simply make us smarter by providing us with more information, it was written to change our relationship with God and the way we are supposed to live.

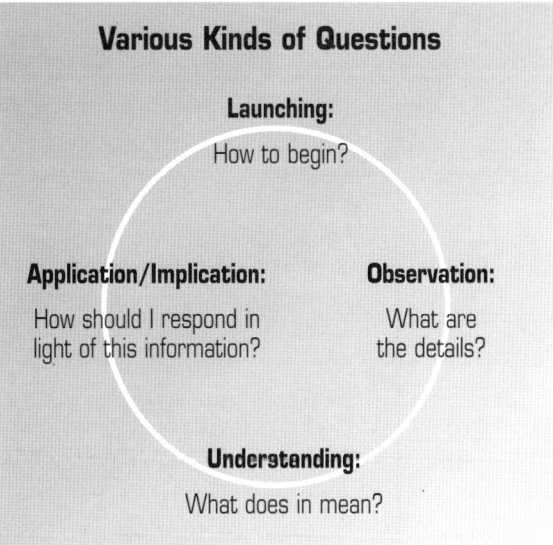

Various Kinds of Questions

Launching:
How to begin?

Application/Implication:
How should I respond in light of this information?

Observation:
What are the details?

Understanding:
What does in mean?

In the following illustration we introduce one other type of question, the Launching Question. Launching questions are by nature a little different than the above three and they simply provide an answer to the question, "How shall I begin, or kick off the discussion of this chapter or this section of material?" It can be something as simple as, "In these next six questions on the gifts of the

Holy Spirit what stood out to you?" These launching questions are usually only needed either at the beginning of the evening or the beginning of a new section of material.

Various Types of Understanding Question Formats

As mentioned previously it is helpful both for variety and stimulation to use various understanding question formats. You will find that you will naturally use two or three formats more than the others. So it is helpful once or twice during each bible study booklet to review this list and to try to integrate some variety. Here are nine formats you can use:

Questions of *Value*: This format uses adjectives like "most," "main," "major," "least," "primary," etc., words that cause the answerer to assign value to a set of facts. Because the question is formed in terms of what is most valuable *to them,* they do not need to fear giving the wrong answer or having to defend their answer. They are simply sharing what *they* perceive is most valuable. However, because in any group the participants will have multiple opinions, this question format tends to elicit additional opinions and the reasoning behind them, thus generating interaction. Here are two examples of this format:

1. What to you is the *least* important aspect of evangelization?

2. How would you state the *major* truth of this chapter?

Questions of *Feeling*: This format is especially valuable when facilitating a group in which one or more participants may feel somewhat insecure about sharing. If you ask them a question that requires them to give a definitive answer, they will often freeze up and simply mumble an, "I don't know." However, if you handle the same material with a feeling question, they usually will be quite comfortable telling you how they feel. Frequently, you can then move them from a feeling question right into the question, "What then do you think it means?" Here are two examples of this format:

1. Why do you *feel* that we often want "an eye for an eye, a tooth for a tooth" or revenge, when we have been wronged?

2. How did you *respond emotionally* to this passage on the roles of the husband and wife?

Questions of *Relationship*: This question format deals less with stimulating discussion and more with revealing understanding. It tends to force group members back into the material you are using, to rethink and rediscover some truth they overlooked. It calls for answerers to discover a connection between facts. Often when the *connection* is discovered, such as a cause-and-effect relationship between two concepts, the Holy Spirit opens our minds to deeper more meaningful truths. Here are two examples:

1. What is the *relationship* between forgiveness and bitterness according to this text?
2. What is the *connection* between the disciples having received power after having received the Holy Spirit, and their role as witnesses?

Questions of *Identification*: This question format asks people to look at a story or narrative that involves several people or several elements and to identify with one of them and explain why. It can be very self revealing, enabling participants to draw a personal connection to the bible story or passage.

1. For instance in the story of the prodigal son(s) with whom do you identify?
2. In the four types of soil Jesus mentions which soil is most like you?

Questions of *Example*: This type of question requires a person to take a significant concept and look into their own world and own experience for something or someone who illustrates the concept. This is a helpful way to make the abstract concrete.

1. Would someone give me an example of "loving your neighbor"?
2. Describe a situation that would demonstrate when it is appropriate to "turn the other cheek".

Questions of *Similarities* or *Opposites*: This question format forces people to clarify concepts by contrasting or comparing two things. This process magnifies the characteristics of one or the other by looking at them along side of one another.

1. What is the difference between "grace" and "works"?
2. What differences do you see between Jesus' response to the woman taken in adultery and the people's response?
3. How are the needs of an infant and a new believer similar?

Questions of *Summary:* This type of question asks the participants to consider all that has been read or said and restate it in a conclusive and comprehensive way. This is a helpful process at the end of a chapter or section of material to make sure that the main point of the chapter or section is not lost in the details.

1. How would you summarize the lessons learned from this chapter?
2. Please summarize this parable's lesson about "forgiveness."

Questions of *Definition:* Many errors of interpretation begin because people impose on words a meaning different than the one the writers of Scripture intended. In addition the meaning of some words have changed or been expanded over time, consequently it is very helpful to clarify the meaning of key words. (A bible dictionary, concordance, or lexicon are helpful tools in this process.)

1. How would you define "fruitfulness"?
2. What does the word "shepherd" convey to you?
3. What is "eternal life" besides living forever?

Questions of *Explanation:* Questions of explanation require the answerer to put into their own words a complex concept.

1. Explain what you think is meant by the quotation on page 16.
2. How would you explain the statement that the "kingdom of God is within you"?

Lastly, here are three principles that will serve you well if you implement them in your role as facilitator of a small-group discussion.

K.I.S.S. Principle: "Keep It Simple, Stupid" provides a very blunt reminder that most people appreciate functioning on a basic academic level. When you use highfalutin theological and ecclesiastical terms, you may sound intellectual, but you do not enable others to relate to what you are saying. Most profound statements are simple statements that are profound in their simplicity. So when you compose your discussion group questions, compose short, simple sentences free of undefined theological or ecclesiastical terms.

When you ask a question of the group, and one or more people asks you to repeat the question, it usually indicates that you have stated a question that is too long and complex. Often by the time you get to the end of your question people will have forgotten the first part of the question and invariably will ask, "Would you repeat that?" If you have a complex concept that you would like to introduce with a question, try composing a couple of short questions, rather than a longer, complex sentence.

Dead-enders: A dead-end question is either one that results in either a "yes" or "no" answer or one with a pre-conceived answer. Invariably these begin with a helping verb such as "don't," "do," "does," "is," "are," "was," "were," "could," "would," "should," etc. When a sentence begins with one of these words, the answer always results in "yes" or "no" and stifles discussion. For example, "Don't you think this is a good suggestion?" If you want to generate discussion, you should practice writing your questions without beginning them with a helping verb. Restate questions like the one above into one such as, "What do you think of this suggestion?"

The question with a pre-conceived answer would be a question that implies only one answer is correct, for instance, "What lesson is Jesus teaching in this section?" The implication is that there is only one lesson taught. This leaves people trying to guess what the facilitator is referring to, and leaves the facilitator having to say, "No, that's not it." A better question would be, "What lessons do you see in this passage?," thus allowing the participants to share the lessons they see rather then simply trying to guess the one the facilitator had in mind.

Don't preach: Because you are also learning a lot and feel passionate about some of the things you believe in, it is easy to appear as though you are on a soapbox preaching at the others. As you know, most people do not appreciate being preached at, and if they become too uncomfortable with someone preaching at them, they will simply extricate themselves from the situation and stop attending.

You can share some really intense concepts without preaching by avoiding pronouns such as "you" and "your." Instead share the same concept using "I" and "we." People will still be impacted by what you say but without feeling preached at. As you read the following two examples, you will see how this works.

(a) Preaching—"You need to take this passage about being transformed seriously. If you really want to be transformed, you will begin really studying God's Word and allow the Holy Spirit to renew your mind."

(b) Sharing—"As I read this passage about transformation, I realized that I need to really take this seriously. If I want to allow myself to be transformed, I will need to get serious about studying God's Word and allow the Holy Spirit to really renew my mind."

Paragraph (a) sounds like preaching and like you are pointing out their failures and needs. On the other hand, paragraph (b), though making the same points just as strongly, sounds like a non-threatening testimony. The second statement communicates the issues just as clearly, and though others will feel equally challenged by your sharing, no one will feel personally lambasted.

The value of well prepared and timely understanding questions is that;

- They enable people to think more thoroughly about an issue.
- They provide stimulation and interest
- They draw others into the discussion
- They help clarify difficult material
- They reveal where people are in their thinking

Things to remember when facilitating a discussion;

- Never tell when you can ask—Telling shortcuts their learning process by giving them answers they didn't have to think about.

- Never answer when you can refer them to the others—Referring questions that arise to others in the group enables everyone to think through the issue more thoroughly, and learn to articulate their thinking. It also prevents you from becoming the "answer guru."

- Never answer when you don't know—Otherwise you are giving out un-thought through answers, and they will spot a phony in a minute. Set the example of humility by simply saying, "I don't know the answer, but I'll find out and let you know," or better yet, "I don't know but would you due some research, talk with the pastor, and come back and tell us what you learned?"

One **Place Where It Happened**

Holy Apostles Parish, in Colorado Springs, CO —Discovering Community Through Small-Groups

Hank and Rose Stamps was one of those who was invited to attend a small-group orientation meeting after mass at Holy Apostles Parish. The pastor, Fr. Paul Wicker, invited interested parishioners to attend the orientation and consider joining a small-group. Hank and Rose Stamps attended along with several other parishioners. "We had been praying about small-group bible studies for and with adults who wanted to grow in their faith and we were glad to attend. We were impressed with what the speaker had to say at this short meeting, and along with fifteen other people joined Holy Apostles first Small-group Catholic Community. Due to the facilitator's faith, encouragement, bible knowledge and persistence plus a great sense of humor, our group grew in love of studying the word of God and in fellowship with one another.

"We enjoyed this small-group community so much that we eventually became facilitators for our own group in our home. We discovered

Rose and Hand Stamps

that being facilitators meant that we needed to study much harder and do much more research in order to be able to lead the group. We have grown so much in our bible knowledge and in our faith through these communities. We have also met and grown in fellowship with all the people who have been involved with us in these groups."

After leading their Small Catholic Community for about a year other people started branching off and forming their own small-groups, which in turn branched off and formed others. For instance Mike and Billie Sue Gonzales were so impacted by their increased understanding of Scripture that they were motivated to receive small-group facilitator training and begin their own bible study. The love, community, and caring environment demonstrated through Mike and Billie Sue's small-group became a model for others and illustrated the principle that much of the success of a weekly small-group bible study takes place in the relationships that exist outside of the weekly meeting. Mike contracted and fought a battle with cancer over the ensuing years. This small-group not only remained cohesive but provided tremendous love and service to Mike and Billie Sue. When Mike and Billie Sue could not be present to facilitate the bible study discussion because of Mike's illness, members of the group filled in and the small-group continued without interruption. Today with Mike looking on from heaven, Billie Sue continues to facilitate small-groups.

Hank and Rose explain, "Since joining the first group we have learned to love the Word of God so much that we start every day with scripture study. We use a Catholic study booklet entitled *Living Faith* which has the daily mass readings with a short commentary on one of the readings for the day. We find this starts our day with an awareness of God in our lives. Another program that we have used is *Reflecting On Sunday's Readings*. This is a bible study that can be accessed and downloaded for free through the Emmaus Journey web page. This program has all three cycles for the Sunday readings with added commentaries and questions that can be studied the week before Sunday mass. We find this so helpful when we attend mass to be prepared to hear the word of God and understand it more fully. This study can be used individually or by family groups. It has been used by Small Catholic Communities with much success as have other bible studies from Emmaus Journey. Consequently, participants are developed with a Catholic perspective."

There have been a lot of benefits from the small-groups at Holy Apostles and one of the most enjoyable has been the way in which relationships are built and friendships formed. These friendships have been long lasting and carry over into other aspects of life in the parish. Perhaps there is no easier way to generate community within a parish than through small-group bible studies.

Holy Apostles Parish, and Fr. Paul Wicker recognized earlier than some the value of small-group bible studies to shape and form Catholics in their faith. Couples like Hank and Rose Stamps, after having first experienced the value of small-group bible studies and receiving the necessary training to become excellent discussion group facilitators have had a profound impact on other parishoners. They have consistently invited their fellow parishioners, year after year, to discover the joy and to experience the affect of knowing Christ through sacred Scripture.

Practical Considerations

Getting Acquainted Exercise

When a small-group first begins it is usually made up of people who know each other to varying degrees, from knowing each other very well to complete unfamiliarity. The desire is that good interpersonal communications among the participants develop as soon as possible. One way to enhance that process during the first two or three meetings is to conduct an exercise designed to help them become better acquainted and build the basis of healthy relationships.

Additionally the exercise we are about to explain will enable the participants to break the "silence sound barrier." This sound barrier is the fear that many people have of speaking aloud for the first time in a group. This exercise helps them overcome this inner fear and start becoming more comfortable hearing their own voice speaking aloud in the group. One other benefit is that it expedites learning one another's names.

Introduce the "Getting Acquainted Exercise" by simply explaining to the group what you are going to do, "In the next few minutes we are going to take some time to get acquainted with one another by answering three simple questions:

- What is your name?
- What is your occupation?
- What is your favorite vacation activity?"

The exercise then begins by you the facilitator sharing your answers to these three questions first, and demonstrating to the participants what you want them to do. In addition you will be illustrating by your example the amount of time and detail for which you are looking. Simply say something like, "Since we want everyone to share, why don't I go first so you get an idea of what we are after from each of you, and then we will proceed around the circle to the left (or right)."

As people share their answers to these questions it is important that you occasionally make encouraging comments such as, "That's interesting," or "Thanks for sharing that with us," or "That's great." In addition if you are familiar with the group you can casually reveal a connection one participant has with another that they might not know about. For example, "Oh, you're a tennis player. Did you know that Bill teaches high school tennis?" Or, "You're from Maine, that's great we don't meet many people from Maine out here. If I remember right I think that Sue and Jim were stationed at Dow AFB. Is that right, Jim?" These little connections begin and expedite the process of assimilation. Lastly, remember to smile and be attentive.

You will find that if you do this at the beginning of the first two or three small-group meetings, friendships will form quickly and people will become increasingly comfortable with one another. Here are two additional sets of questions you can use in the second and/or third week.

Second week questions:

- What is your name?
- Where were you raised?
- What is your favorite hobby?

Third week questions:

- What is your name?
- What do you like about your position in your family (youngest, middle-child, etc.)?
- What is your favorite meal?

The Meeting Environment

The first impression people have about the group is your welcoming environment, which is made up of many elements. Greetings at the door, room set-up, and an enfolding group all contribute to creating a welcoming environment. However we want to consider for a moment the meeting room environment. Your meeting room environment helps to create a learning space that is either conducive to learning or detracting from learning. So don't make the mistake of assuming where you meet doesn't matter a lot, it does.

Here are some things which either contribute to a learning environment or distract from it:

1. Dim lights and high temperatures tend to make people drowsy, whereas good lighting and cooler temperatures tend to keep people alert. Additionally, when there is nice weather people often think how nice it would be to meet outside. However, in most groups there are people who will be distracted by direct sunlight (bald heads and fair skin burn easily). The birds, bees, and bugs though pretty and interesting, for many are a distraction. When considering these things remember to think, cooler is better, brighter is better, and inside is better. Be aware of the needs of older people's and of people with disabilities.

2. The host or hostess, not the same person as the facilitator, needs to sit where they can answer the door or phone and tend to children or pets without bothering people or disrupting the group.

3. When it comes to your pets please remember that not everyone is a pet lover. Friendly dogs and cats can be annoying and distracting. Some people feel threatened by a friendly pet, and it seems that invariably pets find and seek out the non-pet lover in the group. Some people are also allergic to animals. So ideally, your pet should be confined to a part of the house or yard other than where you are meeting

4. Metal chairs, sitting on the floor, etc. makes it very difficult to concentrate if you have to sit that way for more than fifteen minutes, unless you are under 18 years old. We have found that it is much better to purchase inexpensive plastic lawn chairs with arm rests on them for more pleasant seating whose discomfort doesn't distract a person's attention.

5. The seats should be arranged in somewhat of a circle since this arrangement encourages interaction. Classroom seating where the facilitator is on one side facing the participants tends to set up a

teacher/teachee relationship which discourages interaction between the members of the group. Instead it causes a more formal relationship where the communication always goes back to the facilitator.

6. Avoid objects such as lamps, flowers, etc., coming between people's eye contact, so that everyone can see each other well. This may involve making a few minor furniture rearrangements. People need to have good eye contact if they are to enjoy the group and be encouraged to participate.

7. Whether to have refreshments or not is always a consideration. If you decide to have refreshments share the responsibility with the people in the group. Make it a point to keep refreshments simple. The objective is to have something that encourages socializing and relationship building, not to provide gourmet food. If one person is an especially good cook and brings something really nice, unless the other participants are reminded to keep it simple, they will be put under tremendous pressure to also make something really nice.

You will also need to determine if you will have refreshments before, during, or after the small group discussion. Our personal preference is to provide a hot and cold drink option at the beginning of the small-group which people can sip on during the discussion, and then to provide a dessert goody after the discussion to encourage people to hang around and talk. You will be surprised at how much ministry will take place during these socializing times.

8. Offer your home as a gift to Christ. When we decided years ago to open our home to ministry we also had to decide how we were going to respond to the inevitable wear and tear that would take place by having a group of people visit our home, week in and week out, year in year out, in all kinds of weather. We knew that inevitably with this much activity in our home that refreshments would be spilled on our rugs and on our furniture. We had to decide whether it was more important to have a home that made a fashion statement or to have a

home that made a hospitality statement. We concluded that people are more important than things. Things will ultimately be destroyed and can be replaced, souls will last for eternity.

These considerations also raise the question of whether you should meet in the parish building or in homes for your small groups. If you can take into account these practical considerations in the rooms within the parish building(s) than it might be an appropriate place to meet. Since most parish facilities are not conducive to this type of non-classroom environment you perhaps should consider meeting in someone's home.

If you chose to rotate meetings from home to home you will need to make an extra effort to help the prospective host understand the above considerations. Usually it is preferable to meet in the same home for the duration of the study you are doing, say for six to ten weeks. In this way directions to the home are not a problem, nor do you end up in a situation where many of the above considerations are overlooked. If you take these few practical steps you will find that people will be able to relax and be comfortable and will then be able to focus all of their attention on the material at hand.

Handling Extensive Text

Some bible studies involve discussing longer sections of written material explaining Scripture, or in some cases small-groups decide to discuss an article, an encyclical or Church writing, or a popular Christian book. Because these kinds of materials usually do not have pre-written small-group questions and because they involve such extensively written text they need to be handled a little differently.

The first thing to point out is that every participant should have their own individual copy of the material. If you allow a couple to share the article, bible studies, encyclical, Church writing, or Christian book, invariably one person of the couple does all of the work and the other simply comes along for a free ride. To have effective discussion every person must become engaged with the material on their own. Even when each person has their own material and has read it in advance, by the time the group comes together to discuss the material, it is not unusual for people to have forgotten much of the content and feel ill prepared to share. Consequently we recommend several steps to overcome this situation.

1. Explain in advance that when they read the material, encyclical, or book they should use a pen or pencil to mark within the text those things that stood out to them. Encourage them to use several kinds of markings to provide variety and to make portions of the text stand out in different ways. For instance they can use:

    - Circles
    - Underlining
    - Brackets [ ]
    - Question mark (?)
    - Astericks (*)
    - Notes in the margin, etc.

Then before discussing a section, give them 30–60 seconds to review what they marked before you begin asking discussion questions.

2. It is also helpful to have the portion you are going to be discussing, or several portions re-read aloud by members of the group. (This is crucial if you are getting ready to discuss material some of them have not read.) The advantage of having participants take turns reading the material aloud is that both the slow readers and the speedy readers end up at the same place at the same time. On the other hand if one person reads the entire article or material to the others it often becomes quite boring and little information is grasped sufficiently enough to discuss. In a similar manner having the participants each read the material silently presents problems with some people taking way too long to read it, while others speed read the material. So we encourage the reading aloud of sections of this kind of material by the group before jumping into the discussion.

Initially when I was exposed to this technique in the early 80's I was convinced it wouldn't work. I was leading a small-group bible study with professional couples and I assumed that they would think this process was too juvenile. To my amazement they loved it and entered into the reading of the paragraphs we were to discuss without missing a beat. Additionally, I have seen some great side benefits from this practice. For instance, poor readers to whom we usually assign a short paragraph, eventually become excellent readers by participating in this way with the group—and actually develop a love for reading outside of the group. One man who literally had eyeglass lenses 3/8 of an inch thick and had to hold the booklet within three inches of his eyes felt very affirmed each week when he was treated no differently than the others and was allowed to read.

Here are several additional benefits of reading the extended paragraphs of material aloud together:

- It continually helps break the sound barrier for those who are more timid about sharing.
- Having just read the material aloud it is more fresh and stimulating than something read several days ago.

- Reading aloud involves more senses and organs—eyes, ears, voice, brain—and consequently makes a deeper impression.

One thing that is helpful to remember is to not quickly jump in and correct a person's pronunciation or reading errors. We all will be conscious of these mistakes and will give the person reading, the benefit of the doubt.

One Place Where It Happened

St. Paul's University Catholic Center, at the University of Wisconsin, Madison—Evangelizing Through Small-Groups

Andre Lesperance explains, "We prize small group bible studies as one of our most effective ministries for outreach and faith-building. Through small groups, students who might not otherwise come to church or get involved are invited to encounter authentic Christian community among their fellow students who are searching for more out of life than college alone has to offer. The most striking example of this that I have encountered is a wild young man named Bob who grew up Catholic but left church behind when he came to college. During his freshman year in the dorms, Bob and his friend decided that it would be fun to get buzzed on alcohol and then attend the Bible study that met on their dorm floor. For mere amusement and mockery, the two of them made this practice a part of their weekly routine. They managed to keep controlled enough for other participants in the small group not to know that they had been drinking, which only added to their amusement. One week, Bob's friend could not make it to Bible study, and Bob didn't want to get drunk on his own. So he decided to go to the small group sober. To his surprise, he still enjoyed it. He found something appealing about the way these students were seeking Jesus Christ together week in and week out. Bob kept going every week, without any alcohol in him. A few months later, Bob attended one of our retreats and made a decision to follow Christ, received the Sacrament of Reconciliation, and is now one of our core student leaders.

Andre Lesperance

"How did this ministry come to be? There have been significant student ministries on the UW campus since the late 1800's, but the recent growth all started from one dynamic small group. In the mid 1990's, Tim and Sandy Kruse, friends of the St. Paul's community, began hosting a weekly small group in their home for anyone interested. Several college students attended, as well as various other adult friends. This group encountered the Lord together in a powerful way. Each week they would study the Scriptures, pray and sing praise together, growing in their convictions for spreading the good news of Jesus Christ. Finally, in 1999 the pastor of St. Paul's invited Tim to launch small groups on the UW-Madison Campus. Tim recruited several of the attendees to join him in leading small groups for one academic year in the dorms on campus. Their hope was to attract participants and then select student leaders from these participants to continue the ministry the following years. This effort was clearly blessed by God, as the recruitment of the fall of 1999 produced more interested college students than Tim and his crew knew what to do with. They were able, though, to find even more leaders for that initial year, and small groups were launched with astonishing success.

"We believe that any ministry ought not just to be measured *vertically*—counting the participants, but also *horizontally*—how it flows from and leads to other ministries vital to the overall vision of the church. While that initial year enjoyed significant vertical success in great numbers of students coming to small groups, it also was hugely successful in the horizontal dimension. Daily mass attendance went from 5 or 10 students to around 50 over the next two years. Retreats went from 25 people to 150 over the three years since launching small groups. After the initial year of small groups led by Tim and his crew, student leaders stepped up to continue the ministry and receive ongoing training. St. Paul's continues today to flourish in large part due the way in which the Lord uses these small group bible studies. It is truly an exciting work.

"In addition to evangelizing and 'pre-evangelizing' one of the goals of small group Bible studies is to seek together how to live out the truths revealed in the Scriptures. We train our small group leaders not to leave discussions suspended in philosophical speculation, but to elicit practical, relevant applications for the path of daily discipleship."

The Catholics at the University of Wisconsin student ministry have discovered that whether your goal is to get non-believers thinking, or to get believers formed in their faith, small-groups provide an ideal fomat.

Handling Discussion-Group Obstacles

I f you have led many small-group discussions, you realize that no matter how thoroughly you pray and prepare, inevitably some obstacles arise which hinder effective discussion. This section discusses common types of obstacles and suggests ways to handle them.

You can avoid most obstacles by putting into practice the small-group dynamics discussed here within this comprehensive training material. For instance, good communication during the promotion and recruiting process for a small-group will attract people who will provide minimum difficulties when participating in the group's discussions. When you fail to practice principles of good communication during the start-up of a group, you inevitably have to deal with problems like absences, dropouts, and poor participation later.

The most foundational aspect of dealing with all of these situations is to develop a genuine love for those participating and to relate to them in love and graciousness. For the most part, this will mean that when a problem or obstacle to discussion arises, you, as the facilitator, will take the responsibility for the situation rather than shifting the blame to the participants. This attitude will express itself in your being quick to say, "I'm sorry," and to sacrificially bear the burden of the misunderstanding. It is helpful to remember that we are Christ's body, the hands, feet, mouth, etc., through which he express his life and love. As a facilitator, you also have the privilege of sharing in his suffering in these practical ways.

You will also find that you have a tremendous resource in prayer, and through it you are able to elicit the help of the Holy Spirit. The most powerful methodology you can use to overcome problems and obstacles is having an active prayer life for the small-group you facilitate and the individuals participating in it. The following are eight of the most common discussion-group obstacles people encounter.

Inadequate Participant Preparation: When you encounter this situation, you need to keep in mind that your objective is not to be judgmental but to provide the kind of motivation and encouragement needed, so that in the future the person will better prepare for the discussion. Consequently, you need to avoid a spirit of condemnation, no matter how frequently you encounter this problem. Condemnation will not motivate the person to prepare but may motivate someone to no longer attend.

As mentioned previously this problem is best solved in advance by leading the participants into a group commitment to adequately prepare. During this commitment discussion, it also helps to point out that when a person does not adequately prepare, they defraud not only themselves but also the entire group by withholding their thought-through contributions.

During these preliminary discussions, it also helps to point out to the group that when a person consistently comes unprepared or refuses to participate wholeheartedly, they are making a negative, nonverbal statement about their own spiritual health and attitudes. Often this revelation alone will stimulate them to prepare.

When a person does show up unprepared, commend them for attending rather than skipping the meeting, even though unprepared. At least by attending they can profit by listening to the others discuss the material, and perhaps at some point they will even be able to enter into the discussion. While commending them for coming, also let them know how much more the group would be enriched by their learning and contributions if they had prepared ahead of time.

If the problem persists, arrange a one-on-one meeting with the person to discuss the problem. Begin by taking responsibility and giving them a chance to share any problems they may have. You could say something such as: "Bob, I've noticed that you frequently haven't prepared the material we are to discuss. Is there anything I am doing or the group is doing that contributes to this situation?" Usually, this will disarm the person and they will share freely what *their* problem is.

Communicate to the individual that usually a person gets something out of a discussion in proportion to what they put into the preparation and discussion. Encourage the person to start preparation early in the week, and to make a concerted effort to prepare as the others do.

On the other hand, if several in the group are showing up unprepared, it would help to discuss the problem with the entire group. Review the commitment card, ask for their input (Is the material too difficult? Are the lessons too long or too uninteresting? Or is there something lacking in the facilitation of the discussion?) and elicit a renewal of their commitment to prepare.

Getting Sidetracked: Every group gets sidetracked at one point or another. As the facilitator, you need to be focused but relaxed in pursuing the objective of the discussion material. You will want to provide both freedom and direction to the group discussion without appearing either authoritarian or *laissez faire* in your leadership.

Let's face it. Sometimes the rabbit trails are more fun than the material we are scheduled to discuss. These excursions can be both fun and interesting, and as the discussion-group facilitator, it is important for you to remember that the objective isn't only to take the mountain but also to enjoy the process. After a reasonable amount of time exploring a rabbit trail, acknowledge to the group your responsibility for allowing the group to get off track by saying something such as, "Hey, folks, I need to apologize for letting us get so off track. This discussion has been fun, but let's returns to the subject at hand." Usually, that reminder is enough to move right back into the material at the point where you departed.

Another technique you can use is to suggest that the group table the discussion for now and return to it at a later date. Sometimes it helps to direct them to an imaginary shelf and suggest, "Let's can this topic for now, and put it up on the shelf and bring it back down and reopen it at some point in the future."

Unusual or Incorrect Doctrine: When we are discussing Scripture or Church teachings, we all are concerned about truth and correct doctrine. Unfortunately, sometimes our concern for correct doctrine overrides our concern for an individual and their hunger for truth. Consequently, in our articulation of the truth, often in an uncalled-for forceful and strident way, we pour cold water on the person's desire to learn and express their beliefs for fear that they will be jumped on theologically. The key to handling this situation is to allow the small-group community to provide doctrinal balance without creating division or communicating a judgmental corner on the truth.

Affirm what you can affirm, ignore that which you cannot affirm, and encourage the expression of sound teaching, is a simple guide to keep in mind when facilitating a group. Do not make the mistake of falling into the roll of "doctrinal policeman." It is better to lead the group into discovering the right answer than simply giving them the right answer. This is where your skills in developing questions will serve you well. If participants begin to see your role as one of correcting them doctrinally, your discussion group will quickly dissolve into a monologue.

Acknowledge and affirm the person's contribution with a, "Thanks Dan, that's a new way to express that thought" or "That's interesting. I've never heard that before." Often this is a good time to also add; "Could you elaborate a little?" to make sure you understand what is being said. Then turn to the others in the group and ask, "How did some of the rest of you handle this question?" As you hear contributions that you believe to be more consistent with sound doctrine, reinforce the validity of the answers with a simple comment such as, "That's a great answer! Thanks."

Some differences will not be easily resolved and you should look on these differences as opportunities for growth. Allow lively discussion, but don't allow the discussion to degenerate into an argument. At the appropriate place, rearticulate what you understand are the two positions, and then ask someone who is not directly involved in the discussion to research the answer and report what they find out. If it is a theological issue, encourage them to especially talk with the parish priest and refer to the new Catechism as answers are sought.

Remember that you are forming convictions and values in others and you want them to feel passionate about the things that are important to them—their faith, their values, their families, etc. However, your passion must be balanced by a willingness to love and treat others with courtesy. Group unity is based on our mutual baptism into Christ and on our commitment to some basic core beliefs, not on uniformity in non-essentials.

Overly Talkative Participants: With overly talkative participants the objective is to enable the person to moderate their contribution without squelching their enthusiasm. With this kind of person there are several things you can do to bring them into balance.

Recruit them to help you draw out others. Take them aside and explain, "Sue you really have some great things to share in the group and you share so freely and enthusiastically. Thanks, so much for your participation. Have you noticed though that some people haven't shared very much. I'm wondering if they would share more if they didn't have your sharing to rely on. Could I recruit you to help me draw out the more quite ones by your sharing less frequently so that they might feel the need to fill the empty spaces?" In this way you are inviting the participant to help. Remember to affirm them if they do restrain from excessive talking with words like, "Sue, you did a great job tonight. I knew you had a lot to share but that you were holding back, and I think it worked. We had many more sharing tonight than normal."

Choose a seat next to them. Once the overly talkative person has chosen a seat, choose to sit right next to them. You may have noticed that often the overly talkative person seems to sit right across from you and always catches your eye and jumps in prematurely. By sitting next to them you remove that factor and they can only catch your eye when you purposely turn and look at them.

In addition, by sitting next to them you are able to tactfully use some physical and visual gestures to indicate that they should wait a minute and let someone else speak.

Direct the question to a specific person. If the above suggestions don't work then when you ask a question, or ask someone to read the next question and give their answer, direct your question to a specific person, "Bill, would you read and answer question three?"

Answer in order. An alternative to the one mentioned above is to simply work around the group in order having each in turn share their answers. Unfortunately, this works for one or two sessions but becomes fairly stilted after awhile. So it is a short range rather than a long range solution.

Lastly, if someone is insensitive enough to not pick up your verbal and non-verbal signals, or to not respond to your request to help by curtailing some of their comments, usually they are not so sensitive that they will be hurt by a direct comment like, "Thanks, Sue, but if you don't mind I'd like for some of the others to give us their thoughts since you have already shared a lot."

Overly Quiet Participants: The objective for this type of participant is to insure that they feel included and affirmed, and understand that the group would really value their thoughts and contributions, while allowing the group to be comfortable with their quietness. You can do this by:

Providing extra affirmation. We have seen very timid and quiet participants who have only spoken when specifically called upon blossom into confident sharers due to the affirmation they have received. Little things can really make a difference, like really listening to their answer and then following it with an appropriate statement like, "Mary, what a profound comment. You have gone right to the heart of the passage. You need to share more, there is a lot we can learn from you."

Additionally, in the social time after the discussion, or in one-on-one conversations at church it is helpful to say something like, "Mary, the things you shared last week in the small-group were really good. I wish you would share even more. You seem to have some deep thoughts and we would love to hear more of them." You will be amazed at what a little affirmation will do to bring out the best in people.

Calling on them periodically. It is helpful with the overly quiet individual to call on them at least twice during the evening and to be ready to encourage them to expand on their comment.

Sitting opposite them. This is the opposite technique to what we mentioned on the overly talkative person. By your choosing a seat opposite the quiet person, each time you look up you will catch their eye as you are asking the question and apply a little subtle pressure for them to share by silently saying, "What do you think?"

Allowing them to pass if they prefer not to share. All of these suggestions are designed to *encourage* them to share, not force them to share. So along with these suggestions you need to be willing to give them the time necessary to become comfortable sharing, and until they do to allow them to pass for the time being.

Providing Care for Group Participants: As we mentioned elsewhere a lot that contributes to the success of the small-group are the things which take place outside of the discussion group time and which create a sense of community. Meeting needs and caring for people is one aspect of that process. At the same time trying to meet those needs on your own can both wear you out and undermine community. So the objective is to meet the social and care needs of the participants without burning out the facilitator or neglecting individuals. Here are three things you can do:

Share the care with the group. Invite the participants of the small-group to join with you in helping other participants whether it involves helping someone move, providing a meal when someone is sick, praying for someone, or sitting with someone who is in the hospital, etc. Do not hesitate to specifically ask people to do something which will help another member of the group. If someone is missing for instance, instead of your contacting them to find out how they are doing and to fill them in on what they missed, or on what is happening next week, ask one of the group to contact them about these things and to let you know what they find out.

Provide relationship building activities. Potluck suppers, one-on-one conversations, holiday or birthday festivities, and watching the big games together are just some of the things you can do to generate relationship building activities. Mike and Billie Sue were great examples in this regard. We mentioned them earlier in the story of Holy Apostles small-groups. Their groups were always getting together to help one another or to celebrate some aspect of their lives together. In the ensuing months after Mike's illness, their community thrived even though their favorite facilitator could only occasionally attend, because they had built lasting relationships and had learned how to assume responsibility for their group members.

Be attentive to the person who is being left out. A phenomenon I have disappointingly observed for years is the tendency of Christian people, when they meet in various sized groups to clump together with their friends and leave new people standing there alone with their coffee cup wondering if they fit in. Small-group fellowship after a bible study discussion tends to be no different. The new people are often left floundering. As a facilitator one of your objectives is to both seek out and converse with these individuals who are less known and to help assimilate them into the group by inviting other more well known members of the group into conversations with them. When this happens the entire group benefits.

Handling Disruptive Behavior: The objective is to minimize disruptions, so that participants can get the most out of the discussion. Disruptions can take many forms, from the person who is always joking or making a wise crack, to people who begin conversations on the side, or maintain a running commentary while others are talking, etc. There are several things you can do, many of which are less than pleasant but which are necessary if the group is to function without distraction.

Discuss appropriate behavior in advance. I have found it helpful to talk a little in the opening orientation meeting about things which contribute to having an effective group. In the course of sharing it is appropriate to talk about some of the kinds of participant behavior which negatively affects the group. For instance, I'll point out that we want everyone to attend the discussion group each week even when they have a hard day or hard week. However, I'll also mention that we need to learn how to manage our attitude and spirit in the midst of the difficult day or week so that others in the group don't become so aware of our negative attitudes and sighs that they are sidetracked from the lesson at hand. This is also a place where you can comment, "It is great to have a good sense of humor and a ready wit, but we will need to curtail it in the group so that we are not having fun at another's expense or having so much fun that others are distracted from the discussion." Preventive maintenance works wonders.

Talk one-on-one to the person about the affect they are having. If the above doesn't do the trick, ask to get a cup of coffee with the person whose behavior is disruptive and explain to them the affect their behavior is having on the group. Affirm how valuable they are as a participant in the group but ask them to confine their comments and behavior to that which is helpful.

Be graciously direct. The previous comments on the insensitivity of a person to not catch the verbal and non-verbal cues applies here as well. If the above two suggestions are not working, in the midst of the discussion as the disruptive behavior takes place it is then appropriate to graciously and pleasantly—but firmly, say, "Mel, I love your sense of humor but it really is out of place here. Please restrain your comments." Or, "Jane and Martha, I'm being distracted by your conversations on the side while we are discussing this material. Please join us rather than having a private discussion." This direct approach should be used only when other things have failed, however, don't let your group be highjacked by people who are impolite.

Sit alongside to moderate actions. Enough has been said about how to position yourself next to or across from people in order that eye contact and physical and visual cues can be utilized. Those same principles apply in this situation.

Emotional Release: We are after all, emotional creatures. In the course of facilitating your small-group you are going to touch on a host of different subjects, some of which will deeply and emotionally touch the core of some participants. Also, some people will show up at the discussion carrying a lot of emotional baggage with them which sometimes is released in the midst of the discussion, or just due to some caring comment. This is not a *bad* thing but it can be an obstacle to the discussion. The objective is to welcome these emotions as a precious moment of vulnerability which can lead to healing and conversion, without making the person self-conscious or without abandoning the purpose of the small-group. When they occur:

Reassure the group that showing emotions is okay. This can be done with something as simple as saying, "Thanks, Henry, for letting us know what you are feeling and experiencing—that takes a great deal of courage." If you are thrown by an emotional outburst or emotional release it will communicate to the group that it is not okay to be real.

Don't feel a need to "fix" it. Most things that would warrant an emotional outpouring are not something that we can fix, and in reality most people are not looking for someone to fix it but for someone to listen and understand. So once someone has expressed their wrought up emotions simply thank them for bringing us into their feelings and for sharing them with us. Turn to the group and suggest, "Before we continue on, perhaps we should pause for a few minutes and pray for Henry, or perhaps pray silently for Henry. Then after a few minutes of prayer, (or silent prayer) I'll close by praying aloud and then we can get back to the study." This also gives the person who was emotional a few minutes to regain composure.

Divert attention from the person to the material and the group. Often when someone shares emotionally like this, they are no sooner finished then they regret having been so vulnerable and feel very self-conscious. This is a good time to take the spotlight off of them and turn it on to you or on to the group. This can be done by simply asking the question, "Have any of you ever felt like Henry? I know I have." Then you can just take a few minutes of sharing from the group. After a few minutes simply say something like, "Thanks again Henry for being so vulnerable. Let's get back into the study with question 4, etc.?"

Most problems within the discussion can be avoided by good preparation and good communication ahead of time. Those that crop up are often a blessing in disguise and actually raise the level of community and bonding. Welcome them as opportunities rather than fear them as foes. If God has called you to facilitate the group he has done so knowing full well your gifts, personality, and ability. By the power of the Holy Spirit he will equip you to meet the needs of those within your small-group.

One Place Where It Happened

St. Gertrude Catholic Church, Cincinnati, OH— Men Meeting with Men

Kevin Lynch notes that in the late 1980's, long before Promise Keepers and similar men's ministries developed, God began a work among men in Cincinnati, Ohio. Four men recognized the need for Catholic men to pray together and share their faith. Out of their initial efforts of contacting men and explaining this vision there now exists almost 200 Catholic men's fellowship groups in the Cincinnati region. St. Gertrude Catholic Church's men's fellowship was one of the first of these.

Kevin Lynch, Founder of the St. Gertrude men's fellowship explains, "The group that formed at St. Gertrude's is a good illustration of how these small men's fellowship groups work and look. In fact, many of the fellowship groups are formed along similar lines, and several serve as incubators for other new groups. These incubator groups allow potential leaders to attend sessions with a mature men's group and then initiate a new, similar gathering of men in their home or adjacent parish."

Kevin Lynch

Additionally, leadership training is not left to chance. "St. Gertrude Parish formed a leadership team so that responsibilities were shared and a format was adopted that remains to this very day. It is important to note that this is a dynamic team so responsibilities are rotated and men become competent in a number of areas of leadership. This is especially important for learning the facilitator's role. This leader must present a fresh, encouraging and effective tone to the discussion so that all participants feel valued."

St. Gertrude Parish's men begin with light refreshments, usually a robust song, and prayers and petitions by the prayer leader in which any of the men can join. The facilitator leads men in a discussion of the Scripture passages and Catechism selections they are scheduled to discuss. "This format encourages men to be honest with one another and to openly share what is going on in their lives. It is important that a non-judgmental attitude prevail among the men, which means that trust must also be high among the men."

"Topics vary but an effort is made to make sure that they relate to issues more germane to men and the sort of issues men grapple with on a daily basis. One area that arouses intense discussion centers on the spiritual aspects of fatherhood. For example: 'How did your father model a prayer life for you?' and/or 'What does it mean to you that your Heavenly Father loves you unconditionally?' and 'How do you pass that on to your children?'

"We have found a number of guides to be helpful. We often begin a group by using *SIGNPOSTS*, published by The Word Among Us Press. *SIGNPOSTS* contains 52 topics that focus on relationships, and other male oriented topics, with provocative discussion questions tied to the Scripture and Catechism references. One of our men recently commented that 'The beauty of SIGNPOSTS lies in the fact that once we work our way through it we can start over using it again because our thinking changes over the course of the 52 sessions!'

"A number of Emmaus Journey publications have also served as excellent resources for our group over the years," Kevin explains. *"Embracing The Kingdom* and, more recently, *Living In The Power Of The Holy Spirit* have fueled many a fine session among our men. Books like this not only prove to be helpful discussion starters but excellent tools for learning about – and enriching – our Catholic faith."

Does a parish benefit from men's small-groups like Kevin has talked about? Well two indicators of their value is 1) do they produce active parishoners who assume responsibility for the work of the ministry, and 2) does the parish pastor view them as an asset or a liability. Both criterion are being met Kevin says, "Many members of the St. Gertrude men's group have assumed other roles within the parish as a result of their participation in the men's fellowship group. ... Our Pastor, Fr. Ken Letoile, actively encourages the group, participates when he can, and 'loves having a men's fellowship group in my parish!'"

What a good deal! Men meeting with and forming men, "Fundamentally to seek a personal relationship with Jesus by bonding with each other, in an atmosphere of trust, as they pray, share and minister to one another. The basic aim is to help men grow in holiness." This is an idea whose time has arrived.

A Recap

Throughout this training tool we have listed and explained several principles of facilitating small-groups and have alluded to or implied several others. In these final paragraphs we want to succinctly reiterate those things which contribute either to the failure or success of a small-group.

- Have Unclear Expectations—nothing kills a small-group faster than having people participate for the wrong reasons and attending expecting something totally different.

- Inexperienced and untrained leaders—usually are unable to maximize either the potential of the group or the significance of the material. It is a wise investment to train facilitators.

- Ineffective materials—tend to curtail enthusiasm and discussion. Take the time to seek out and review the material you are considering to insure that the writer effectively enables people to discover truth.

- Being unprepared—if anything is worth doing it is worth doing right. If God has called you to be a small-group facilitator prepare in such a way that will bring honor to him and skill to the group.

- Talking instead of asking questions or listening—small-group discussion isn't about us, the facilitator, and how much we know. It is all about helping others discover God and the truths he has for them, and enabling them to articulate these new found truths in a cogent manner.

- Start on time and end on time—people will love you for it, it's respectful of them, and will enable the participants to plan wisely.

- Practice good human relationship skills—facilitating a small-group is 90% simply knowing how to relate to a variety of people in a loving and gracious way, while providing direction and incentives for them to share what they are learning. The converse is true if instead you simply view the small-group as an activity, or "ministry" and not as a set of relationships to savor and enjoy. Your propensity for failing will greatly increase.

- Smile and be pleasant, laugh, express appreciation and enjoyment—this could both become the most enjoyable experience of your life and lead you into some of the deepest friendships.

- Be positive, gracious and enthusiastic, develop a "you" attitude—remember whom you represent. You are not only the facilitator, you not only represent the parish, but you are Christ's body for facilitating that group. Your actions, skills, and attitudes should communicate to those participating what Christ thinks of them.

- Show non-verbal interest—a warm hand-shake, a ready smile, a gracious hug, and a helping hand are just a few ways that people sub-consciously interpret your verbal messages. Make sure that you use both the visual and the verbal to communicate that they are VERY important to God and to you.

- Let them save face—when a problem arises take the responsibility for it, whether you feel you were the cause or not. Be quick to apologize remembering that Proverbs reminds us that a soft answer turns away wrath.

- Relax, don't be formal and stiff.

- Be honest, sharing your feelings, hurts, and needs. People don't expect you to be perfect—simply real. People can learn from your failures as well as your successes.

- Avoid religious jargon.

- Have fun.

Conclusion

Being a small-group discussion facilitator is akin to being a mountain guide. Your role is to help others scale the mountain of God's love and truth, and not simply to climb the mountain yourself and tell others about it. You want the people in your group to grow in every aspect of their lives, whether it is as spiritual individuals, as holy marriage partners and parents, as Catholic workers, or as church leaders. You want to help others have a first-hand experience with Christ rather than a second-hand faith. Consequently, God is very interested in your role as facilitator and is committed to helping you succeed. So thank God for the privilege of serving in this way, and dedicate your life to growing in skill and competence as a small-group discussion facilitator.

Additional small-group resources are available at www.emmausjourney.org, the Emmaus Journey web page.

About the Author

Rich Cleveland and his wife Gail have been involved full-time in ministry for thirty-eight years. For several years Rich served as the director of Small Christian Communities at Holy Apostles Parish in Colorado Springs, and is a current member of the Diocese's Metro North Region Pastoral Council and Director of the Holy Apostles Men's Breakfast. In addition Rich serves as a Trustee for the National Fellowship of Catholic Men and is a member of the Executive Council. Rich and Gail have three married sons.

Rich also is the Founder and Director of Emmaus Journey: A Catholic Ministry of Evangelization and Discipleship. Through this ministry, Rich and Gail have published several Scripture-based Catholic small group studies, and he is the author of several bestselling Catholic Bible studies published by The Word Among Us Press. Rich publishes *Reflecting on Sunday's Readings,* a small-group study based on each Sunday's Mass readings, which can be downloaded for free from the Emmaus Journey website at www.emmausjourney.org.

Rich has served as a speaker and seminar leader at numerous Christian conferences and conventions, including the Raleigh, NC Diocesan Leadership Conference, the National Council of Catholic Evangelization, St. Paul's Institute of Catholic Evangelization, the Franciscan University of Steubenville's Men's Conferences, Journey of a Lifetime Conference, The Catherine of Siena Institute, The Evangelical Catholic Institute, and the National Fellowship of Catholic Men's Leaders Conference.

Emmaus Journey

Emmaus Journey is a Catholic evangelization and discipleship ministry that is conducted primarily in and through Catholic parishes. Emmaus Journey has embraced Goal One of *Go and Make Disciples:* "To bring about in all Catholics such an enthusiasm for their faith that, in living their faith in Jesus, they freely share it with others."

Emmaus Journey endeavors to accomplish this goal by:

- Helping Catholics who only occasionally practice their faith or who are nominal in their commitment, to experience conversion to Christ.

- Encouraging individuals to experience transformation in Christ as they grow in understanding and commitment to Scripture and the Church's teachings.

- Mobilizing Catholics to become actively involved in sharing their faith among the non-religious and in the process of forming disciples.

- **By providing high quality, thoroughly Catholic, practical small-group bible study materials,** evangelization and discipleship resources, seminars, and ministry events that help equip Catholic parishes and individuals to do the ministry of evangelization and discipleship.

Emmaus Journey ministry resources can be found on the internet at **www.emmausjourney.org,**

Contact Information:
Email: **info@emmausjourney.org**
Telephone: 719-599-0448
Mail: PO Box 63587, Colorado Springs, CO 80962

Please visit www.emmausjourney.org for our latest materials.

Emmaus Journey
Catholic Small-Group Resources

The vision of *Emmaus Journey* is to help Catholics mature in Christ, to grow in their understanding and commitment to sacred Scripture and Church teachings, and to fan into flame people's commitment to prayer and evangelization.

Emmaus Journey contributes to this goal by helping parish leaders inaugurate small-groups and small Christian communities within their parishes; assisting in the training of small-group facilitators; and providing practical small-group resources.

Emmaus Journey small-group materials integrate Scripture study with meaningful support materials from Church teachings and Catholic leaders, using a practical topical approach. These studies provide an effective addition to existing adult formation resources and are available at a reasonable cost.

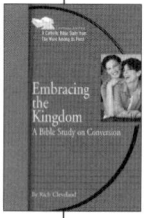
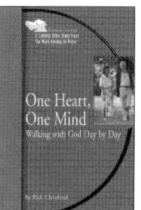
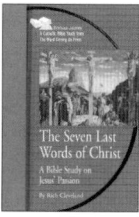
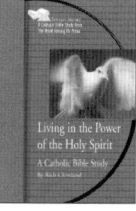

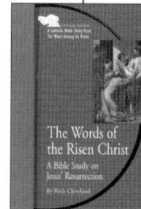

In addition *Emmaus Journey* provides effective formation materials and training resources in various multi-media formats. Decades of ministry experience in evangelization and disciple-making are reflected in these practical training tools. These resources will impact your life and enhance your ministry, and can be found on the Emmaus Journey web page.

Please visit www.emmausjourney.org for our latest materials.